She Energy
Tracking Journal

A self-awareness
guide to your
natural energy cycle

JESSICA TERLICK

the kind press

Copyright © 2022 Jessica Terlick
First published by the kind press, 2022

All rights reserved. No part of this book may be reproduced, stored in a retrieval system or transmitted in any form or by any means, electronic, mechanical photocopying, recording, or otherwise, without written permission from the author and publisher.

This publication contains the opinions and ideas of its author. It is intended to provide helpful and informative material on the subjects addressed in the publication. While the publisher and author have used their best efforts in preparing this book, the nature of the material in this book is general comment only. It is sold with the understanding that the author and publisher are not engaged in rendering advice or any other kind of personal professional service in the book. In the event that you use any of the information in this book for yourself, the author and the publisher assume no responsibility for your actions.

Cover design: Miladinka Milic
Internal design: Nicola Matthews, Nikki Jane Design

Cataloguing-in-Publication entry is available from the National Library Australia.

ISBN: 978-0-6455237-6-8
ISBN: 978-0-6455237-7-5 eBook

Indigenous and Traditional Owners

I wish to acknowledge the Traditional Custodians of the land on which I have written this book, the Whadjuk people. I would like to pay respect to the Elders of the Noongar nation, past, present and future, who have walked and cared for the land. I acknowledge and respect their continuing culture and the contributions made to the life and the land in which I now live.

I would also like to acknowledge the six Indigenous seasons Birak, Bunuru, Djeran, Makuru, Djilba and Kambarang.

A note from the author

Regarding gender identity, I wish to acknowledge non-binary and transgender people, and convey that my use of the word 'she' is not intended to offend anyone. My usage of 'she' refers to feminine energy in which all humans have.

On my use of the word seasons, I understand that those who live closer to the equator do not experience the four seasons as I do. Please note that the seasons are used as a way to communicate and identify the 4 stages of your energy cycle.

Welcome to your She Energy Tracking Journal

A place for your own personal development journey!

How many times have you found yourself wishing for more time or even just time for yourself? Once you have a better understanding of the real you – how you work, what holds you back and what inspires you – it becomes so much easier to be the best version of yourself.

This journal is a tool to help you track your personal cycle in a number of areas, including energy levels, eating patterns and general mood. So when you feel tired and drained for no obvious reason, you will know why. Instead of wishing for more time and energy, you will have a better understanding of how you work, and then utilise the time and energy you have.

Once you are aware of your changing cycles, with a bit of planning you can ensure your day's itinerary doesn't feel overwhelming and there are tasks that you are looking forward to. There will be enjoyment, laughter and productivity!

It's also important to remember that there's no shame in asking for help. See your friends, family and others as part of your 'dream team'; those who will support you to be your best. Please seek professional advice and help at any time you feel you may need it.

So, let's begin, shall we?

Always with a smile,

JESSICA TERLICK

Understanding Cycles

We experience cycles every month and by better understanding them, we can better plan for them.

Does the following sound familiar? You receive an invitation two weeks before a party and you're so excited to attend. Then that weekend arrives and it's now the last thing you feel like doing. Another week you might feel totally on top of everything; you have everything sorted in the home, feel like everyone is happy at the moment and everything feels organised, and you are so pumped that you make a list of tasks for the following week...only to achieve nothing at all.

It's something we all experience, yet we don't stop to ask why. So let's break it down so you can take control of your cycle, rather than letting it rule over you! Your first step is to reconnect with yourself.

These are some questions you will be asking yourself over the course of a cycle:
- What activities do you like to do every week?
- How do your feelings change every week?
- What foods do you crave at different stages of the cycle?

- What are your energy levels from week to week?
- How emotional do you get from week to week?

Challenge the following assumptions:
- When did being busy become something to celebrate?
- Why do we feel like we always need to be doing something and that rest is only something we do when we sleep?

I cover more on this in my workshops and coaching sessions so please reach out at any point to learn more, however by studying yourself and working through this journal you will be able to generally find how your cycle works with the other cycles – moon, menstrual and seasonal.

Enjoy!

Moon Cycle Key

We still don't fully understand the effect the moon has on us, just that it does influence behaviours. Learning how the moon changes and then recording your individual experience at these times can be helpful in understanding your personal rhythms.

New Moon	Consider this the beginning of the cycle. The moon is completely black and this is the time to set your intentions for the month ahead. Dream and set goals.
Waxing Crescent	This represents the beginning of new things. It is the growing stage. Build upon the foundations you put in place during your previous cycle or what you set out to do at the new moon phase.
First Quarter	Really make the most of all your energy! Tick off items on your to-do list.

Waxing Gibbous		You may start to feel more emotional than usual. Take a little time to listen to what your body needs – you may need to slow down to make the most of the next wave of energy coming your way.
Full Moon		The midway point of the moon phase. This is your peak time! You may feel extra emotional or charged so utilise this energy in a positive way. You may have been working non-stop until this point and as the moon phases continue it will be time to slow down and assess where you are at.
Waning Gibbous		Time to start finishing projects, crossing things off your list, dropping unimportant tasks and preparing to have some down (or even hibernation) time.
Last Quarter		Begin resting, reflecting and reassessing what you have achieved in the month.
Waning Crescent		Start preparations for the new moon cycle. Roll with the energy you have over the next four weeks! Utilise the time and energy you have to get the activities you feel like doing according to the time of the month.

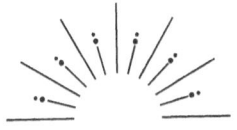

Seasonal Week Key

The moon phases can be described in simpler detail by following the seasons. When you think about the seasons, think about the weather, how you feel, what is happening in nature, how you socialise, what you eat and what activities you do.

NEW MOON AND WAXING CRESCENT

Season
Winter (Days 1-7 of Menstrual Cycle)
Mood
During this time we like to hibernate.
We often stay at home to avoid the colder weather and meals tend to be warming, slow-cooked and hearty.
Nature
In nature, the rain waters your dry earth.
Animals hibernate and rest for when they need to venture out in the warmer months.

FIRST QUARTER AND WAXING GIBBOUS

Season
Spring (Days 8-14 of Menstrual Cycle)
Mood
After locking ourselves away for a couple of months we start to feel like we want to get out of the house and socialise. When the warmer weather appears, we seem to have more energy. Spring cleaning is actually a thing because we have been in our homes for so long we have seen what our habitats contain and want to sort it all out.
Nature
In nature, new sprouts begin to grow. Flowers begin to bloom. It is a new beginning as plants have been dormant and animals have been hibernating. Time to start feeling the warmth and grow!

FULL MOON AND WANING GIBBOUS

Season
Summer (Days 15-21 of Menstrual Cycle)
Mood
It's warm so we like to get outside and enjoy the weather. It's a time to socialise and we tend to prefer eating lighter food.
Nature
Both animals and plants harness the sunshine but too much can cause problems!

LAST QUARTER AND WANING CRESCENT

Season
Autumn (Days 22-28 of Menstrual Cycle)

Mood
We welcome the cooler weather after the warmer months. We have enjoyed socialising but are now looking forward to spending some time at home and the invitations to outings slow down. Trackie pants and TV anyone?

Nature
The leaves begin to fall off the trees and animals prepare for winter.

Moon Cycle and Seasons Cycle

Whichever cycle you are using, start thinking about your personal inclinations and energy levels over the weeks. Refer back to the behavioural questions outlined above. Remember, 'Winter' is the start and is day one. Day one can be the start of your period, the full moon or the new moon. Here is an example of what I personally experience:

WINTER WEEK

Mood

I feel very strong during this time (however, others may have an experience more similar to my 'autumn'). This is my planning week for everything: I put structures in place because in the next two weeks I will have the energy to get them all done. This is a great time to rest and relax more because in doing so, I will have more energy in the weeks to come.

Planning

I prefer not to speak to people because I want to get tasks organised and completed on my own. It is the best time for me to get 'pen and paper' jobs done. I am more creative and intuitive at this time. I always feel like hearty meals. This is the week I feel like calling people and making appointments for the month.

SPRING WEEK

Mood

This is my most energetic time. I make sure I save all my tasks for the month for this week.

Planning

This is my power week. This week I get the most compliments. I feel like eating well, exercising and socialising.

SUMMER WEEK

Mood

This week I know my energy is starting to run out, so I only try to complete the tasks that need to be done. I allow myself to be okay with not getting everything done because being hard on myself is using energy I'd rather spend on the activities I feel like doing.

Planning

This is the week I like trying new recipes. I still feel like socialising. I get the jobs done that I need to. I feel like healthy meals. Everything feels like it is all balanced and I am handling things really well.

AUTUMN WEEK

Mood

This week the leaves are definitely falling off my tree! I am emotional and sensitive. I allow myself to hibernate, rest and relax. I don't push myself too much when exercising and I allow myself to eat a little off track during this time, because I know

I will eat better in the other weeks (so I don't beat myself up about it and just enjoy).

Planning

This week I feel really low on energy. I don't feel like putting in as much effort with my appearance. I cook fast and easy meals. I get pimples, headaches and really want to eat sugar and carbohydrates. I want to get things done but it seems like it takes even longer than usual. So, I schedule a lot of self-care and 'me time' activities during this week.

PLANNING

WINTER WEEK	General observations:	How I feel and my energy level:
	Tasks I enjoy doing or feel like doing:	Tasks I really do not feel like doing during this time:
SPRING WEEK	General observations:	How I feel and my energy level:
	Tasks I enjoy doing or feel like doing:	Tasks I really do not feel like doing during this time:

PLANNING

SUMMER WEEK	General observations:	How I feel and my energy level:
	Tasks I enjoy doing or feel like doing:	Tasks I really do not feel like doing during this time:
AUTUMN WEEK	General observations:	How I feel and my energy level:
	Tasks I enjoy doing or feel like doing:	Tasks I really do not feel like doing during this time:

NOTES

NOTES

NOTES

NOTES

MY ACTION PLAN

Things I would like to do more of:

Things I would like to do less:

Ways I can make this happen:

MY CHALLENGES

Challenges I might come up against:

Ways of dealing with these challenges:

When I am in need of support I will talk to:

When I overcome these challenges I will celebrate by:

Summer

IMPORTANT DATES

	Mon	Tue	Wed	Thu	Fri	Sat	Sun
DECEMBER							

	Mon	Tue	Wed	Thu	Fri	Sat	Sun
JANUARY							

	Mon	Tue	Wed	Thu	Fri	Sat	Sun
FEBRUARY							

SUMMER ACTION PLAN

WINTER WEEK	Energy level (high, medium, low):	
	Activities I like to do in this time:	Activities I prefer not to do in this time:

SPRING WEEK	Energy level (high, medium, low):	
	Activities I like to do in this time:	Activities I prefer not to do in this time:

SUMMER WEEK	Energy level (high, medium, low):	
	Activities I like to do in this time:	Activities I prefer not to do in this time:

AUTUMN WEEK	Energy level (high, medium, low):	
	Activities I like to do in this time:	Activities I prefer not to do in this time:

DECEMBER PLANNER

MONDAY	TUESDAY	WEDNESDAY	THURSDAY

FRIDAY	SATURDAY	SUNDAY

Week:

MOON CYCLE	ENERGY LEVEL

THINGS TO DO THIS WEEK

DAILY MANTRA

DAILY RITUALS

SEASONAL ACTIVITIES

SWEAT SESSIONS

Seasonal Week:

WHAT THIS MEANS FOR ME

MONDAY	TASK		
TUESDAY	TASK		
WEDNESDAY	TASK		
THURSDAY	TASK		
FRIDAY	TASK		
SATURDAY	TASK		
SUNDAY	TASK		

Week:

| MOON CYCLE | ENERGY LEVEL |

THINGS TO DO THIS WEEK

DAILY MANTRA

DAILY RITUALS

SEASONAL ACTIVITIES

SWEAT SESSIONS

Seasonal Week:

WHAT THIS MEANS FOR ME

MONDAY	TASK		
TUESDAY	TASK		
WEDNESDAY	TASK		
THURSDAY	TASK		
FRIDAY	TASK		
SATURDAY	TASK		
SUNDAY	TASK		

Week:

| MOON CYCLE | ENERGY LEVEL |

THINGS TO DO THIS WEEK

DAILY MANTRA

DAILY RITUALS

SEASONAL ACTIVITIES

SWEAT SESSIONS

Seasonal Week:

WHAT THIS MEANS FOR ME

MONDAY	TASK		
TUESDAY	TASK		
WEDNESDAY	TASK		
THURSDAY	TASK		
FRIDAY	TASK		
SATURDAY	TASK		
SUNDAY	TASK		

Week:

| MOON CYCLE | ENERGY LEVEL |

THINGS TO DO THIS WEEK

DAILY MANTRA

DAILY RITUALS

SEASONAL ACTIVITIES

SWEAT SESSIONS

Seasonal Week:

WHAT THIS MEANS FOR ME

MONDAY	TASK		
TUESDAY	TASK		
WEDNESDAY	TASK		
THURSDAY	TASK		
FRIDAY	TASK		
SATURDAY	TASK		
SUNDAY	TASK		

Week:

MOON CYCLE	ENERGY LEVEL

THINGS TO DO THIS WEEK

DAILY MANTRA

DAILY RITUALS

SEASONAL ACTIVITIES

SWEAT SESSIONS

Seasonal Week:

WHAT THIS MEANS FOR ME

MONDAY	TASK		
TUESDAY	TASK		
WEDNESDAY	TASK		
THURSDAY	TASK		
FRIDAY	TASK		
SATURDAY	TASK		
SUNDAY	TASK		

JANUARY PLANNER

MONDAY	TUESDAY	WEDNESDAY	THURSDAY

FRIDAY	SATURDAY	SUNDAY

Week:

MOON CYCLE	ENERGY LEVEL

THINGS TO DO THIS WEEK

DAILY MANTRA

DAILY RITUALS

SEASONAL ACTIVITIES

SWEAT SESSIONS

Seasonal Week:

WHAT THIS MEANS FOR ME

MONDAY	TASK		
TUESDAY	TASK		
WEDNESDAY	TASK		
THURSDAY	TASK		
FRIDAY	TASK		
SATURDAY	TASK		
SUNDAY	TASK		

Week:

| MOON CYCLE | ENERGY LEVEL |

THINGS TO DO THIS WEEK

DAILY MANTRA

DAILY RITUALS

SEASONAL ACTIVITIES

SWEAT SESSIONS

Seasonal Week:

WHAT THIS MEANS FOR ME

MONDAY	TASK		
TUESDAY	TASK		
WEDNESDAY	TASK		
THURSDAY	TASK		
FRIDAY	TASK		
SATURDAY	TASK		
SUNDAY	TASK		

Week:

MOON CYCLE	ENERGY LEVEL

THINGS TO DO THIS WEEK

DAILY MANTRA

DAILY RITUALS

SEASONAL ACTIVITIES

SWEAT SESSIONS

Seasonal Week:

WHAT THIS MEANS FOR ME

MONDAY	TASK			
TUESDAY	TASK			
WEDNESDAY	TASK			
THURSDAY	TASK			
FRIDAY	TASK			
SATURDAY	TASK			
SUNDAY	TASK			

Week:

| MOON CYCLE | ENERGY LEVEL |

THINGS TO DO THIS WEEK

DAILY MANTRA

DAILY RITUALS

SEASONAL ACTIVITIES

SWEAT SESSIONS

Seasonal Week:

WHAT THIS MEANS FOR ME

MONDAY	TASK			
TUESDAY	TASK			
WEDNESDAY	TASK			
THURSDAY	TASK			
FRIDAY	TASK			
SATURDAY	TASK			
SUNDAY	TASK			

Week:

MOON CYCLE	ENERGY LEVEL

THINGS TO DO THIS WEEK

DAILY MANTRA

DAILY RITUALS

SEASONAL ACTIVITIES

SWEAT SESSIONS

Seasonal Week:

WHAT THIS MEANS FOR ME

MONDAY	TASK			
TUESDAY	TASK			
WEDNESDAY	TASK			
THURSDAY	TASK			
FRIDAY	TASK			
SATURDAY	TASK			
SUNDAY	TASK			

FEBRUARY PLANNER

MONDAY	TUESDAY	WEDNESDAY	THURSDAY

FRIDAY	SATURDAY	SUNDAY

Week:

MOON CYCLE	ENERGY LEVEL

THINGS TO DO THIS WEEK

DAILY MANTRA

DAILY RITUALS

SEASONAL ACTIVITIES

SWEAT SESSIONS

Seasonal Week:

WHAT THIS MEANS FOR ME

MONDAY	TASK		
TUESDAY	TASK		
WEDNESDAY	TASK		
THURSDAY	TASK		
FRIDAY	TASK		
SATURDAY	TASK		
SUNDAY	TASK		

Week:

MOON CYCLE	ENERGY LEVEL

THINGS TO DO THIS WEEK

DAILY MANTRA

DAILY RITUALS

SEASONAL ACTIVITIES

SWEAT SESSIONS

Seasonal Week:

WHAT THIS MEANS FOR ME

MONDAY	TASK		
TUESDAY	TASK		
WEDNESDAY	TASK		
THURSDAY	TASK		
FRIDAY	TASK		
SATURDAY	TASK		
SUNDAY	TASK		

Week:

| MOON CYCLE | ENERGY LEVEL |

THINGS TO DO THIS WEEK

DAILY MANTRA

DAILY RITUALS

SEASONAL ACTIVITIES

SWEAT SESSIONS

Seasonal Week:

WHAT THIS MEANS FOR ME

MONDAY	TASK			
TUESDAY	TASK			
WEDNESDAY	TASK			
THURSDAY	TASK			
FRIDAY	TASK			
SATURDAY	TASK			
SUNDAY	TASK			

Week:

MOON CYCLE	ENERGY LEVEL

THINGS TO DO THIS WEEK

DAILY MANTRA

DAILY RITUALS

SEASONAL ACTIVITIES

SWEAT SESSIONS

Seasonal Week:

WHAT THIS MEANS FOR ME

MONDAY	TASK		
TUESDAY	TASK		
WEDNESDAY	TASK		
THURSDAY	TASK		
FRIDAY	TASK		
SATURDAY	TASK		
SUNDAY	TASK		

Week:

MOON CYCLE	ENERGY LEVEL

THINGS TO DO THIS WEEK

DAILY MANTRA

DAILY RITUALS

SEASONAL ACTIVITIES

SWEAT SESSIONS

Seasonal Week:

WHAT THIS MEANS FOR ME

MONDAY	TASK		
TUESDAY	TASK		
WEDNESDAY	TASK		
THURSDAY	TASK		
FRIDAY	TASK		
SATURDAY	TASK		
SUNDAY	TASK		

NOTES

Lead by example and inspire others at the same time

- JESSICA TERLICK

SUMMER REFLECTION

Things I didn't do enough of:

Things I did too much of:

Ways I can change this:

MY CHALLENGES

Challenges I came up against:

Ways I dealt with these challenges:

Things I could have done better:

Things I am really proud of:

Autumn

IMPORTANT DATES

MARCH	Mon	Tue	Wed	Thu	Fri	Sat	Sun

APRIL	Mon	Tue	Wed	Thu	Fri	Sat	Sun

MAY	Mon	Tue	Wed	Thu	Fri	Sat	Sun

AUTUMN ACTION PLAN

WINTER WEEK	Energy level (high, medium, low):	
	Activities I like to do in this time:	Activities I prefer not to do in this time:
SPRING WEEK	Energy level (high, medium, low):	
	Activities I like to do in this time:	Activities I prefer not to do in this time:
SUMMER WEEK	Energy level (high, medium, low):	
	Activities I like to do in this time:	Activities I prefer not to do in this time:
AUTUMN WEEK	Energy level (high, medium, low):	
	Activities I like to do in this time:	Activities I prefer not to do in this time:

MARCH PLANNER

MONDAY	TUESDAY	WEDNESDAY	THURSDAY

FRIDAY	SATURDAY	SUNDAY

Week:

| MOON CYCLE | ENERGY LEVEL |

THINGS TO DO THIS WEEK

DAILY MANTRA

DAILY RITUALS

SEASONAL ACTIVITIES

SWEAT SESSIONS

Seasonal Week:

WHAT THIS MEANS FOR ME

MONDAY	TASK		
TUESDAY	TASK		
WEDNESDAY	TASK		
THURSDAY	TASK		
FRIDAY	TASK		
SATURDAY	TASK		
SUNDAY	TASK		

Week:

MOON CYCLE	ENERGY LEVEL

THINGS TO DO THIS WEEK

DAILY MANTRA

DAILY RITUALS

SEASONAL ACTIVITIES

SWEAT SESSIONS

Seasonal Week:

WHAT THIS MEANS FOR ME

MONDAY	TASK		
TUESDAY	TASK		
WEDNESDAY	TASK		
THURSDAY	TASK		
FRIDAY	TASK		
SATURDAY	TASK		
SUNDAY	TASK		

Week:

MOON CYCLE	ENERGY LEVEL

THINGS TO DO THIS WEEK

DAILY MANTRA

DAILY RITUALS

SEASONAL ACTIVITIES

SWEAT SESSIONS

Seasonal Week:

WHAT THIS MEANS FOR ME

MONDAY	TASK		
TUESDAY	TASK		
WEDNESDAY	TASK		
THURSDAY	TASK		
FRIDAY	TASK		
SATURDAY	TASK		
SUNDAY	TASK		

Week:

| MOON CYCLE | ENERGY LEVEL |

THINGS TO DO THIS WEEK

DAILY MANTRA

DAILY RITUALS

SEASONAL ACTIVITIES

SWEAT SESSIONS

Seasonal Week:

WHAT THIS MEANS FOR ME

MONDAY	TASK		
TUESDAY	TASK		
WEDNESDAY	TASK		
THURSDAY	TASK		
FRIDAY	TASK		
SATURDAY	TASK		
SUNDAY	TASK		

Week:

| MOON CYCLE | ENERGY LEVEL |

THINGS TO DO THIS WEEK

DAILY MANTRA

DAILY RITUALS

SEASONAL ACTIVITIES

SWEAT SESSIONS

Seasonal Week:

WHAT THIS MEANS FOR ME

MONDAY	TASK		
TUESDAY	TASK		
WEDNESDAY	TASK		
THURSDAY	TASK		
FRIDAY	TASK		
SATURDAY	TASK		
SUNDAY	TASK		

APRIL PLANNER

MONDAY	TUESDAY	WEDNESDAY	THURSDAY

FRIDAY	SATURDAY	SUNDAY

Week:

MOON CYCLE	ENERGY LEVEL

THINGS TO DO THIS WEEK

DAILY MANTRA

DAILY RITUALS

SEASONAL ACTIVITIES

SWEAT SESSIONS

Seasonal Week:

WHAT THIS MEANS FOR ME

MONDAY	TASK			
TUESDAY	TASK			
WEDNESDAY	TASK			
THURSDAY	TASK			
FRIDAY	TASK			
SATURDAY	TASK			
SUNDAY	TASK			

Week:

MOON CYCLE	ENERGY LEVEL

THINGS TO DO THIS WEEK

DAILY MANTRA

DAILY RITUALS

SEASONAL ACTIVITIES

SWEAT SESSIONS

Seasonal Week:

WHAT THIS MEANS FOR ME

MONDAY	TASK		
TUESDAY	TASK		
WEDNESDAY	TASK		
THURSDAY	TASK		
FRIDAY	TASK		
SATURDAY	TASK		
SUNDAY	TASK		

Week:

| MOON CYCLE | ENERGY LEVEL |

THINGS TO DO THIS WEEK

DAILY MANTRA

DAILY RITUALS

SEASONAL ACTIVITIES

SWEAT SESSIONS

Seasonal Week:

WHAT THIS MEANS FOR ME

MONDAY	TASK		
TUESDAY	TASK		
WEDNESDAY	TASK		
THURSDAY	TASK		
FRIDAY	TASK		
SATURDAY	TASK		
SUNDAY	TASK		

Week:

MOON CYCLE	ENERGY LEVEL

THINGS TO DO THIS WEEK

DAILY MANTRA

DAILY RITUALS

SEASONAL ACTIVITIES

SWEAT SESSIONS

Seasonal Week:

WHAT THIS MEANS FOR ME

MONDAY	TASK		
TUESDAY	TASK		
WEDNESDAY	TASK		
THURSDAY	TASK		
FRIDAY	TASK		
SATURDAY	TASK		
SUNDAY	TASK		

Week:

| MOON CYCLE | ENERGY LEVEL |

THINGS TO DO THIS WEEK

DAILY MANTRA

DAILY RITUALS

SEASONAL ACTIVITIES

SWEAT SESSIONS

Seasonal Week:

WHAT THIS MEANS FOR ME

MONDAY	TASK		
TUESDAY	TASK		
WEDNESDAY	TASK		
THURSDAY	TASK		
FRIDAY	TASK		
SATURDAY	TASK		
SUNDAY	TASK		

MAY PLANNER

MONDAY	TUESDAY	WEDNESDAY	THURSDAY

FRIDAY	SATURDAY	SUNDAY

Week:

| MOON CYCLE | ENERGY LEVEL |

THINGS TO DO THIS WEEK

DAILY MANTRA

DAILY RITUALS

SEASONAL ACTIVITIES

SWEAT SESSIONS

Seasonal Week:

WHAT THIS MEANS FOR ME

MONDAY	TASK		
TUESDAY	TASK		
WEDNESDAY	TASK		
THURSDAY	TASK		
FRIDAY	TASK		
SATURDAY	TASK		
SUNDAY	TASK		

Week:

| MOON CYCLE | ENERGY LEVEL |

THINGS TO DO THIS WEEK

DAILY MANTRA

DAILY RITUALS

SEASONAL ACTIVITIES

SWEAT SESSIONS

Seasonal Week:

WHAT THIS MEANS FOR ME

MONDAY	TASK		
TUESDAY	TASK		
WEDNESDAY	TASK		
THURSDAY	TASK		
FRIDAY	TASK		
SATURDAY	TASK		
SUNDAY	TASK		

Week:

MOON CYCLE	ENERGY LEVEL

THINGS TO DO THIS WEEK

DAILY MANTRA

DAILY RITUALS

SEASONAL ACTIVITIES

SWEAT SESSIONS

Seasonal Week:

WHAT THIS MEANS FOR ME

MONDAY	TASK		
TUESDAY	TASK		
WEDNESDAY	TASK		
THURSDAY	TASK		
FRIDAY	TASK		
SATURDAY	TASK		
SUNDAY	TASK		

Week:

MOON CYCLE	ENERGY LEVEL

THINGS TO DO THIS WEEK

DAILY MANTRA

DAILY RITUALS

SEASONAL ACTIVITIES

SWEAT SESSIONS

Seasonal Week:

WHAT THIS MEANS FOR ME

MONDAY	TASK		
TUESDAY	TASK		
WEDNESDAY	TASK		
THURSDAY	TASK		
FRIDAY	TASK		
SATURDAY	TASK		
SUNDAY	TASK		

Week:

MOON CYCLE	ENERGY LEVEL

THINGS TO DO THIS WEEK

DAILY MANTRA

DAILY RITUALS

SEASONAL ACTIVITIES

SWEAT SESSIONS

Seasonal Week:

WHAT THIS MEANS FOR ME

MONDAY	TASK		
TUESDAY	TASK		
WEDNESDAY	TASK		
THURSDAY	TASK		
FRIDAY	TASK		
SATURDAY	TASK		
SUNDAY	TASK		

NOTES

True joy comes when you inspire, encourage and guide someone else on a path that benefits him or her

- ZIG ZIGLAR

AUTUMN REFLECTION

Things I didn't do enough of:

Things I did too much of:

Ways I can change this:

MY CHALLENGES

Challenges I came up against:

Ways I dealt with these challenges:

Things I could have done better:

Things I am really proud of:

Winter

IMPORTANT DATES

JUNE	Mon	Tue	Wed	Thu	Fri	Sat	Sun

JULY	Mon	Tue	Wed	Thu	Fri	Sat	Sun

AUGUST	Mon	Tue	Wed	Thu	Fri	Sat	Sun

WINTER ACTION PLAN

WINTER WEEK

Energy level (high, medium, low):

Activities I like to do in this time:

Activities I prefer not to do in this time:

SPRING WEEK

Energy level (high, medium, low):

Activities I like to do in this time:

Activities I prefer not to do in this time:

SUMMER WEEK

Energy level (high, medium, low):

Activities I like to do in this time:

Activities I prefer not to do in this time:

AUTUMN WEEK

Energy level (high, medium, low):

Activities I like to do in this time:

Activities I prefer not to do in this time:

JUNE PLANNER

MONDAY	TUESDAY	WEDNESDAY	THURSDAY

FRIDAY	SATURDAY	SUNDAY

Week:

MOON CYCLE	ENERGY LEVEL

THINGS TO DO THIS WEEK

DAILY MANTRA

DAILY RITUALS

SEASONAL ACTIVITIES

SWEAT SESSIONS

Seasonal Week:

WHAT THIS MEANS FOR ME

MONDAY	TASK		
TUESDAY	TASK		
WEDNESDAY	TASK		
THURSDAY	TASK		
FRIDAY	TASK		
SATURDAY	TASK		
SUNDAY	TASK		

Week:

| MOON CYCLE | ENERGY LEVEL |

| THINGS TO DO THIS WEEK |

| DAILY MANTRA |

| DAILY RITUALS |

| SEASONAL ACTIVITIES |

| SWEAT SESSIONS |

Seasonal Week:

WHAT THIS MEANS FOR ME

Day	Task		
MONDAY	TASK		
TUESDAY	TASK		
WEDNESDAY	TASK		
THURSDAY	TASK		
FRIDAY	TASK		
SATURDAY	TASK		
SUNDAY	TASK		

Week:

| MOON CYCLE | ENERGY LEVEL |

THINGS TO DO THIS WEEK

DAILY MANTRA

DAILY RITUALS

SEASONAL ACTIVITIES

SWEAT SESSIONS

Seasonal Week:

WHAT THIS MEANS FOR ME

MONDAY	TASK		
TUESDAY	TASK		
WEDNESDAY	TASK		
THURSDAY	TASK		
FRIDAY	TASK		
SATURDAY	TASK		
SUNDAY	TASK		

Week:

| MOON CYCLE | ENERGY LEVEL |

THINGS TO DO THIS WEEK

DAILY MANTRA

DAILY RITUALS

SEASONAL ACTIVITIES

SWEAT SESSIONS

Seasonal Week:

		WHAT THIS MEANS FOR ME	

MONDAY	TASK		

TUESDAY	TASK		

WEDNESDAY	TASK		

THURSDAY	TASK		

FRIDAY	TASK		

SATURDAY	TASK		

SUNDAY	TASK		

Week:

| MOON CYCLE | ENERGY LEVEL |

THINGS TO DO THIS WEEK

DAILY MANTRA

DAILY RITUALS

SEASONAL ACTIVITIES

SWEAT SESSIONS

Seasonal Week:

WHAT THIS MEANS FOR ME

MONDAY	TASK		
TUESDAY	TASK		
WEDNESDAY	TASK		
THURSDAY	TASK		
FRIDAY	TASK		
SATURDAY	TASK		
SUNDAY	TASK		

JULY PLANNER

MONDAY	TUESDAY	WEDNESDAY	THURSDAY

FRIDAY	SATURDAY	SUNDAY

Week:

| MOON CYCLE | ENERGY LEVEL |

THINGS TO DO THIS WEEK

DAILY MANTRA

DAILY RITUALS

SEASONAL ACTIVITIES

SWEAT SESSIONS

Seasonal Week:

WHAT THIS MEANS FOR ME

MONDAY	TASK		
TUESDAY	TASK		
WEDNESDAY	TASK		
THURSDAY	TASK		
FRIDAY	TASK		
SATURDAY	TASK		
SUNDAY	TASK		

Week:

MOON CYCLE	ENERGY LEVEL

THINGS TO DO THIS WEEK

DAILY MANTRA

DAILY RITUALS

SEASONAL ACTIVITIES

SWEAT SESSIONS

Seasonal Week:

WHAT THIS MEANS FOR ME			

MONDAY	TASK		
TUESDAY	TASK		
WEDNESDAY	TASK		
THURSDAY	TASK		
FRIDAY	TASK		
SATURDAY	TASK		
SUNDAY	TASK		

Week:

| MOON CYCLE | ENERGY LEVEL |

THINGS TO DO THIS WEEK

DAILY MANTRA

DAILY RITUALS

SEASONAL ACTIVITIES

SWEAT SESSIONS

Seasonal Week:

WHAT THIS MEANS FOR ME

MONDAY	TASK		
TUESDAY	TASK		
WEDNESDAY	TASK		
THURSDAY	TASK		
FRIDAY	TASK		
SATURDAY	TASK		
SUNDAY	TASK		

Week:

| MOON CYCLE | ENERGY LEVEL |

THINGS TO DO THIS WEEK

DAILY MANTRA

DAILY RITUALS

SEASONAL ACTIVITIES

SWEAT SESSIONS

Seasonal Week:

WHAT THIS MEANS FOR ME

MONDAY	TASK		
TUESDAY	TASK		
WEDNESDAY	TASK		
THURSDAY	TASK		
FRIDAY	TASK		
SATURDAY	TASK		
SUNDAY	TASK		

Week:

| MOON CYCLE | ENERGY LEVEL |

THINGS TO DO THIS WEEK

DAILY MANTRA

DAILY RITUALS

SEASONAL ACTIVITIES

SWEAT SESSIONS

Seasonal Week:

WHAT THIS MEANS FOR ME

MONDAY	TASK			
TUESDAY	TASK			
WEDNESDAY	TASK			
THURSDAY	TASK			
FRIDAY	TASK			
SATURDAY	TASK			
SUNDAY	TASK			

AUGUST PLANNER

MONDAY	TUESDAY	WEDNESDAY	THURSDAY

FRIDAY	SATURDAY	SUNDAY

Week:

| MOON CYCLE | ENERGY LEVEL |

THINGS TO DO THIS WEEK

DAILY MANTRA

DAILY RITUALS

SEASONAL ACTIVITIES

SWEAT SESSIONS

Seasonal Week:

WHAT THIS MEANS FOR ME

MONDAY	TASK		
TUESDAY	TASK		
WEDNESDAY	TASK		
THURSDAY	TASK		
FRIDAY	TASK		
SATURDAY	TASK		
SUNDAY	TASK		

Week:

MOON CYCLE

ENERGY LEVEL

THINGS TO DO THIS WEEK

DAILY MANTRA

DAILY RITUALS

SEASONAL ACTIVITIES

SWEAT SESSIONS

Seasonal Week:

WHAT THIS MEANS FOR ME

MONDAY	TASK		
TUESDAY	TASK		
WEDNESDAY	TASK		
THURSDAY	TASK		
FRIDAY	TASK		
SATURDAY	TASK		
SUNDAY	TASK		

Week:

| MOON CYCLE | ENERGY LEVEL |

THINGS TO DO THIS WEEK

DAILY MANTRA

DAILY RITUALS

SEASONAL ACTIVITIES

SWEAT SESSIONS

Seasonal Week:

WHAT THIS MEANS FOR ME

MONDAY	TASK		
TUESDAY	TASK		
WEDNESDAY	TASK		
THURSDAY	TASK		
FRIDAY	TASK		
SATURDAY	TASK		
SUNDAY	TASK		

Week:

| MOON CYCLE | ENERGY LEVEL |

THINGS TO DO THIS WEEK

DAILY MANTRA

DAILY RITUALS

SEASONAL ACTIVITIES

SWEAT SESSIONS

Seasonal Week:

WHAT THIS MEANS FOR ME

MONDAY	TASK		
TUESDAY	TASK		
WEDNESDAY	TASK		
THURSDAY	TASK		
FRIDAY	TASK		
SATURDAY	TASK		
SUNDAY	TASK		

Week:

| MOON CYCLE | ENERGY LEVEL |

THINGS TO DO THIS WEEK

DAILY MANTRA

DAILY RITUALS

SEASONAL ACTIVITIES

SWEAT SESSIONS

Seasonal Week:

WHAT THIS MEANS FOR ME

MONDAY	TASK		
TUESDAY	TASK		
WEDNESDAY	TASK		
THURSDAY	TASK		
FRIDAY	TASK		
SATURDAY	TASK		
SUNDAY	TASK		

NOTES

When you recover or discover something that nourishes your soul and brings joy; care enough about yourself to make room for it in your life

- JEAN SINODA BOLEN

WINTER REFLECTION

Things I didn't do enough of:

Things I did too much of:

Ways I can change this:

MY CHALLENGES

Challenges I came up against:

Ways I dealt with these challenges:

Things I could have done better:

Things I am really proud of:

Spring

IMPORTANT DATES

	Mon	Tue	Wed	Thu	Fri	Sat	Sun
SEPTEMBER							

	Mon	Tue	Wed	Thu	Fri	Sat	Sun
OCTOBER							

	Mon	Tue	Wed	Thu	Fri	Sat	Sun
NOVEMBER							

SPRING ACTION PLAN

WINTER WEEK

Energy level (high, medium, low):

Activities I like to do in this time:

Activities I prefer not to do in this time:

SPRING WEEK

Energy level (high, medium, low):

Activities I like to do in this time:

Activities I prefer not to do in this time:

SUMMER WEEK

Energy level (high, medium, low):

Activities I like to do in this time:

Activities I prefer not to do in this time:

AUTUMN WEEK

Energy level (high, medium, low):

Activities I like to do in this time:

Activities I prefer not to do in this time:

SEPTEMBER PLANNER

MONDAY	TUESDAY	WEDNESDAY	THURSDAY

FRIDAY	SATURDAY	SUNDAY

Week:

| MOON CYCLE | ENERGY LEVEL |

THINGS TO DO THIS WEEK

DAILY MANTRA

DAILY RITUALS

SEASONAL ACTIVITIES

SWEAT SESSIONS

Seasonal Week:

WHAT THIS MEANS FOR ME

MONDAY	TASK		
TUESDAY	TASK		
WEDNESDAY	TASK		
THURSDAY	TASK		
FRIDAY	TASK		
SATURDAY	TASK		
SUNDAY	TASK		

Week:

MOON CYCLE

ENERGY LEVEL

THINGS TO DO THIS WEEK

DAILY MANTRA

DAILY RITUALS

SEASONAL ACTIVITIES

SWEAT SESSIONS

Seasonal Week:

WHAT THIS MEANS FOR ME

MONDAY	TASK		
TUESDAY	TASK		
WEDNESDAY	TASK		
THURSDAY	TASK		
FRIDAY	TASK		
SATURDAY	TASK		
SUNDAY	TASK		

Week:

MOON CYCLE	ENERGY LEVEL

THINGS TO DO THIS WEEK

DAILY MANTRA

DAILY RITUALS

SEASONAL ACTIVITIES

SWEAT SESSIONS

Seasonal Week:

WHAT THIS MEANS FOR ME

MONDAY	TASK		
TUESDAY	TASK		
WEDNESDAY	TASK		
THURSDAY	TASK		
FRIDAY	TASK		
SATURDAY	TASK		
SUNDAY	TASK		

Week:

MOON CYCLE | ENERGY LEVEL

THINGS TO DO THIS WEEK

DAILY MANTRA

DAILY RITUALS

SEASONAL ACTIVITIES

SWEAT SESSIONS

Seasonal Week:

WHAT THIS MEANS FOR ME

MONDAY	TASK		
TUESDAY	TASK		
WEDNESDAY	TASK		
THURSDAY	TASK		
FRIDAY	TASK		
SATURDAY	TASK		
SUNDAY	TASK		

Week:

| MOON CYCLE | ENERGY LEVEL |

THINGS TO DO THIS WEEK

DAILY MANTRA

DAILY RITUALS

SEASONAL ACTIVITIES

SWEAT SESSIONS

Seasonal Week:

WHAT THIS MEANS FOR ME

MONDAY	TASK		
TUESDAY	TASK		
WEDNESDAY	TASK		
THURSDAY	TASK		
FRIDAY	TASK		
SATURDAY	TASK		
SUNDAY	TASK		

OCTOBER PLANNER

MONDAY	TUESDAY	WEDNESDAY	THURSDAY

FRIDAY	SATURDAY	SUNDAY

Week:

MOON CYCLE	ENERGY LEVEL

THINGS TO DO THIS WEEK

DAILY MANTRA

DAILY RITUALS

SEASONAL ACTIVITIES

SWEAT SESSIONS

Seasonal Week:

WHAT THIS MEANS FOR ME

MONDAY	TASK		
TUESDAY	TASK		
WEDNESDAY	TASK		
THURSDAY	TASK		
FRIDAY	TASK		
SATURDAY	TASK		
SUNDAY	TASK		

Week:

MOON CYCLE	ENERGY LEVEL

THINGS TO DO THIS WEEK

DAILY MANTRA

DAILY RITUALS

SEASONAL ACTIVITIES

SWEAT SESSIONS

Seasonal Week:

WHAT THIS MEANS FOR ME			

MONDAY	TASK		
TUESDAY	TASK		
WEDNESDAY	TASK		
THURSDAY	TASK		
FRIDAY	TASK		
SATURDAY	TASK		
SUNDAY	TASK		

Week:

| MOON CYCLE | ENERGY LEVEL |

THINGS TO DO THIS WEEK

DAILY MANTRA

DAILY RITUALS

SEASONAL ACTIVITIES

SWEAT SESSIONS

Seasonal Week:

WHAT THIS MEANS FOR ME

MONDAY	TASK		
TUESDAY	TASK		
WEDNESDAY	TASK		
THURSDAY	TASK		
FRIDAY	TASK		
SATURDAY	TASK		
SUNDAY	TASK		

Week:

| MOON CYCLE | ENERGY LEVEL |

THINGS TO DO THIS WEEK

DAILY MANTRA

DAILY RITUALS

SEASONAL ACTIVITIES

SWEAT SESSIONS

Seasonal Week:

WHAT THIS MEANS FOR ME

MONDAY	TASK		
TUESDAY	TASK		
WEDNESDAY	TASK		
THURSDAY	TASK		
FRIDAY	TASK		
SATURDAY	TASK		
SUNDAY	TASK		

Week:

MOON CYCLE	ENERGY LEVEL

THINGS TO DO THIS WEEK

DAILY MANTRA

DAILY RITUALS

SEASONAL ACTIVITIES

SWEAT SESSIONS

Seasonal Week:

WHAT THIS MEANS FOR ME

MONDAY	TASK		
TUESDAY	TASK		
WEDNESDAY	TASK		
THURSDAY	TASK		
FRIDAY	TASK		
SATURDAY	TASK		
SUNDAY	TASK		

NOVEMBER PLANNER

MONDAY	TUESDAY	WEDNESDAY	THURSDAY

FRIDAY	SATURDAY	SUNDAY

Week:

| MOON CYCLE | ENERGY LEVEL |

| THINGS TO DO THIS WEEK |

| DAILY MANTRA |

| DAILY RITUALS |

| SEASONAL ACTIVITIES |

| SWEAT SESSIONS |

Seasonal Week:

WHAT THIS MEANS FOR ME

MONDAY	TASK		
TUESDAY	TASK		
WEDNESDAY	TASK		
THURSDAY	TASK		
FRIDAY	TASK		
SATURDAY	TASK		
SUNDAY	TASK		

Week:

MOON CYCLE	ENERGY LEVEL

THINGS TO DO THIS WEEK

DAILY MANTRA

DAILY RITUALS

SEASONAL ACTIVITIES

SWEAT SESSIONS

Seasonal Week:

WHAT THIS MEANS FOR ME

MONDAY	TASK		
TUESDAY	TASK		
WEDNESDAY	TASK		
THURSDAY	TASK		
FRIDAY	TASK		
SATURDAY	TASK		
SUNDAY	TASK		

Week:

MOON CYCLE	ENERGY LEVEL

THINGS TO DO THIS WEEK

DAILY MANTRA

DAILY RITUALS

SEASONAL ACTIVITIES

SWEAT SESSIONS

Seasonal Week:

WHAT THIS MEANS FOR ME

MONDAY	TASK		
TUESDAY	TASK		
WEDNESDAY	TASK		
THURSDAY	TASK		
FRIDAY	TASK		
SATURDAY	TASK		
SUNDAY	TASK		

Week:

| MOON CYCLE | ENERGY LEVEL |

THINGS TO DO THIS WEEK

DAILY MANTRA

DAILY RITUALS

SEASONAL ACTIVITIES

SWEAT SESSIONS

Seasonal Week:

		WHAT THIS MEANS FOR ME	

MONDAY	TASK		

TUESDAY	TASK		

WEDNESDAY	TASK		

THURSDAY	TASK		

FRIDAY	TASK		

SATURDAY	TASK		

SUNDAY	TASK		

Week:

MOON CYCLE	ENERGY LEVEL

THINGS TO DO THIS WEEK

DAILY MANTRA

DAILY RITUALS

SEASONAL ACTIVITIES

SWEAT SESSIONS

Seasonal Week:

WHAT THIS MEANS FOR ME

Day	Task		
MONDAY	TASK		
TUESDAY	TASK		
WEDNESDAY	TASK		
THURSDAY	TASK		
FRIDAY	TASK		
SATURDAY	TASK		
SUNDAY	TASK		

NOTES

I learned to always take on things I'd never done before. Growth and Comfort do not coexist

- GINNI ROMETTY

SPRING REFLECTION

Things I didn't do enough of:

Things I did too much of:

Ways I can change this:

MY CHALLENGES

Challenges I came up against:

Ways I dealt with these challenges:

Things I could have done better:

Things I am really proud of:

About the Author

Jessica Terlick is an energetic presenter and empowerment coach who has been working in education for over a decade. She supports women and children in their personal development journeys through workshops, speaking events, online programs and coaching.

Spreading positive affirmations, Jessica provides women the space to recognise and harness their unique superpowers by prioritising self-care through time management, organisation skills, intention and reflection.

SheEnergy™ is for women who know they deserve more in life! Using the tools Jessica has outlined in *She Energy*, women can learn to utilise their natural feminine cycle to cultivate more time and energy.

Resources

Join our community, receive free materials!
You are invited to follow @jessicaterlick and join our *She Energy* community via www.jessicaterlick.com.au where you can also access free materials, including journals, affirmation cards and vision board cards — and more tools to support you along the way.

She Energy Membership
Explore *She Energy* further alongside this book, access the *She Energy* membership at www.jessicaterlick.com.au/membership

- www.jessicaterlick.com.au
- @jessicaterlick.leadandinspirecommunity
- @jessicaterlick

www.ingramcontent.com/pod-product-compliance
Lightning Source LLC
Chambersburg PA
CBHW030256010526
44107CB00053B/1730